A Manual
for
Acolytes

The Duties of the Server
At Liturgical Celebrations

DENNIS G. MICHNO

With illustrations by Richard E. Mayberry

MOREHOUSE-BARLOW COMPANY
Wilton, Connecticut

Appendix A of this book contains "A Form for the Commissioning of Servers at the Altar" from *The Book of Occasional Services*, published by The Church Hymnal Corporation, and used by permission of The Church Pension Fund.

Third Printing

Morehouse-Barlow Co., Inc.
78 Danbury Road
Wilton, Connecticut 06897

ISBN 0-8192-1272-5

Library of Congress Catalog Card Number 80-81096

Printed in the United States of America

To the Glory of God
and in memory of
Harold Louis Wright, Bishop
Robert Lewis Meaney, Priest
& ·
Robert Morgan Gilday

They served, and serve, in love,
with faithfulness and loyalty.

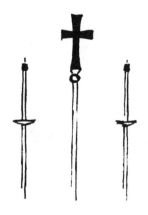

Acknowledgements

My thanks to the Rev. R. DeWitt Mallary, Jr., and the Rev. Charles W. Scott for their patience and helpful suggestions; to Judith de Posz for intensive proofreading and special work on the glossary; to John Hoppe for encouragement and ideas; and to Evelyn P. Mallary, whose gentle push and fervent prayers helped bring this manual to light.

DGM

Table of Contents

Preface

The Book of Common Prayer states, *At all celebrations of the Liturgy, it is fitting that the principal celebrant, whether bishop or priest, be assisted by other priests, and by deacons and lay persons. (BCP, 322 & 354)*

When serving at the altar, one is doing just this: actively assisting the celebrant in the worship of God. This is an important ministry and should be approached with dignity, humility, and care. The server should be well acquainted with the responsibilities and perform the duties with diligence. Sloppiness is to be avoided; stiff or artificial movement is to be avoided; careless or unseemly behavior is to be avoided. In all things, the server must be aware that the purpose in assisting at the altar is "that God may be glorified."

This manual is designed to describe those duties expected of you as a server. *Server* means one who assists—the terms *acolyte, crucifer,* and *thurifer* (as used in this manual) apply to specific responsibilities. No manual can be complete, inasmuch as the custom or use of each parish church varies. However, there are basic directions that apply, governed either by the rubrics of *The Book of Common Prayer* or by tradition. In all things, the specific manner in which one serves and the ceremonial used is determined by the parish priest or the person appointed for this purpose. Most of what will be expected of you can be found in this manual. Also, there may be ceremonies or duties described here that are not part of your parish liturgical life. These are listed as "optional variants" in the main chapter on serving (Chapter 9), and identified by "in some places . . ." in other parts of the manual. Again, your priest will instruct you.

There is absolutely no "right" or "wrong" way to serve. The best rule is that all should be done with dignity and care in the simplest way possible so as not to distract the congregation. Consistent action aids this and helps prevent sloppy carelessness on the one hand and fussiness on the other.

The patron of those who serve at the altar is Vincent, Deacon and Martyr. He lived in the late third century, was martyred in the year 304, and is commemorated in our calendar on January 22. Vincent is remembered for his love of God, his faithfulness to his bishop, and his unswerving loyalty to his responsibilities. These traits—love, faithfulness, and loyalty—are virtues that all who are privileged to serve at the altar should cultivate. Remember: our purpose is rooted in our love of God, our faithfulness is seen in our willingness to serve responsibly, and our loyalty is demonstrated in how carefully we carry out our duties. Love, faithfulness, and loyalty are the virtues we seek to perfect. The server's aim is to be as steadfast as St. Vincent.

This manual may not answer all your questions about serving, but it will assist you in learning the basic principles. Pray, work, and study that you may do all things in love, with faithfulness and loyalty, to the Glory of God.

Dennis G. Michno +
Feast of St. Matthias
February 24, 1981

All Saints Church
New York City

The "MOTTO" used at the title of the preface is from the Rule of St. Benedict: "That in all things God may be glorified."

Part One

An Introduction to Serving

Chapter 1
How To Use This Manual

Part One describes the general procedures, posture, vestments, the way to light and extinguish candles, and includes a check-list for use before the Eucharist.

Part Two (Chapters 8-9) is the most important in that it deals with the basic duties of the server at the Eucharist. First, there is an outline of the Eucharist. Chapter 9 is then divided into four columns: 1) when the celebrant faces the congregation across the altar; 2) when the celebrant faces the cross (with back to the congregation); 3) helpful illustrations; and 4) optional variants. This part of the manual must obviously be adapted to conform with the practice of your own parish church.

Part Three contains a description of the division of the duties if there is more than one server, and then deals with the specific duties of the acolyte,* crucifer, and thurifer.

Part Four contains variants for the Daily Offices and other special liturgies.

This is followed by Appendix A, which is a Form for the Commissioning of Servers, and Appendix B, which is an outline of the Church Year.

At the end there is a Glossary or list of terms used in this manual. If you don't know the meaning of a word, look it up!

Page numbers in italics throughout this manual refer to *The Book of Common Prayer*.

---

*Acolyte is commonly used as a synonym for server. In this manual, for the sake of clarity, acolyte is used specifically for one who carries a torch or candle. Server is the general term used for anyone who assists the celebrant or other officiant.

All who serve at the altar should be familiar with *The Book of Common Prayer* and with the ceremonies and responsibilities described in this manual. Read and study them carefully, and practice so that you are well aware of what is expected of you when you are going to serve.

Chapter 2

The Server's Prayers

"Let love be genuine; hate what is evil, hold fast to what is good; love one another with brotherly affection; outdo one another in showing honor. Never flag in zeal, be aglow with the Spirit, serve the Lord. Rejoice in your hope, be patient in tribulation, be constant in prayer." (Romans 12:9-12)

Before the Service

Be present, Lord Jesus, be present! Grant that I may faithfully and loyally serve you in love and through my service proclaim, "In all things, God be glorified." Amen.

After the Service

Glory to you, Lord Jesus, Glory to you! Grant that as I have served in your presence, so I may witness faithfully and loyally to your love in the world and forever proclaim, "In all things, God be glorified." Amen.

Chapter 3

General Instructions

1 . One who serves at the altar, whether as acolyte, crucifer, or thurifer, must always keep in mind that the attention of the congregation is not to be on those ministering but on the liturgy. Therefore, always move discreetly and quietly—and above all with reverence.

2. Posture:

When *standing*—stand up straight, and if you are carrying a candle or the processional cross make sure that it is straight.

When *kneeling*—put all of your weight on your knees and kneel upright. Do not squat or slouch. It looks terrible!

When *bowing*—There are two types of bows: the solemn and the simple. The solemn bow is used when reverencing the altar, and at other times as directed. The solemn bow is from the waist, inclining the head and shoulders so that if your hands were out in front of you, they would almost touch your knees.

The simple bow, at the name of Jesus and on other occasions of reverence, is made with the head, inclining the shoulders slightly.

One never bows when carrying a candle or the processional cross.

When *genuflecting*—Genuflection (the bending of the knee) is a sign of reverence to the Blessed Sacrament when reserved in an aumbry, tabernacle, or on the altar. It is done simply and with dignity. Don't make it look as if you are falling forward or crouching down!

Standing up straight, bend your right knee until it touches the floor—the left knee will naturally bend a bit—and keep your back straight. This will take practice, but again your actions are not to be a distraction to the congregation.

One never genuflects when carrying a candle or the processional cross.

When *sitting*—sit up straight in the chair, knees together, feet together.

3. What do I do with my hands?

Unless you are carrying something, your hands should always be folded and held above the waist. They should never hang down at your sides or hang folded below the waist.

When sitting, either fold your hands in your lap or place them straight out on your knees with palms down. They are not meant to support your head!

4.　The Sign of the Cross

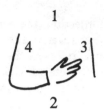

The sign of the cross should always be made reverently and in a dignified manner. Remember, you are signing yourself with the Cross of Christ and this act of devotion should convey that meaning. With your right hand, fingers together, touch your forehead first, then your chest, then your left shoulder, and finally your right shoulder. Keep the hand motions unobtrusive.

The use of the sign of the cross by those serving at the altar is determined by the custom of the parish and the direction of the priest. A good general rule is that when the celebrant makes the sign of the cross, you make the sign of the cross; when the celebrant doesn't, you don't.

5.　Responses

One of your responsibilities is to lead the people in prayers and responses. Therefore, make sure you know them, and say (or sing) them audibly and reverently; don't rush and don't lag behind! Keep the pace set by the celebrant or the congregation.

6.　Walking

Always walk slowly and with dignity when serving at the altar. Your movements should never appear rushed or hurried. But at the same time, stiffness must be avoided. Military steps, square corners, and quick turns are all out of place.

7. Holding a Book

    If you are instructed to hold a book for the prayers of the celebrant, for the reading of the Gospel, during a baptism, wedding, funeral, or a blessing, do so in the following way:

    a.   Make sure the book is opened to the right page.

    b.   Standing in front of the person who is to read, hold the book open.

HOLDING BOOK

**HOLDING BOOK
ON FOREHEAD**

    c.   The bottom of the book should rest in the palms of your hands, but make sure that your fingers are not blocking any of the print. The top of the book should be just below your chin (if you are short and the reader is tall, rest the top of the book on your forehead). The book should be slightly tilted for easy reading.

    d.   If the reader hands you the book unopened, let the reader open it! Hold as above.

    When carrying a book do so in a dignified way—even if it is only your hymnal or prayer book. Hold it above your waist, not down at your side.

8. What do I do with my eyes?

    When one is serving, eyes should always be focused on the action at the altar, on the reader, or on the preacher. It is very distracting to have a server staring into the congregation or at the ceiling. If you don't know where to look, the best thing is to keep your eyes lowered and look at the floor.

Chapter 4

The Vesting of Servers

Those who serve at the altar are regularly vested in either cassock and surplice, amice, alb, and cincture, or cassock-alb.

a. The cassock is worn over street clothes, and should be of such length as to come to the top of the shoes. The surplice, white, with full sleeves, and at least mid-calf in length, is worn over the cassock.

CASSOCK

SURPLICE

b. The amice is worn over the cassock. The alb, a long, white, sleeved garment, is worn over the cassock and amice. The cincture, a long rope, is tied around the waist with a slip knot, and any extra length of rope allowed to hang down the side.

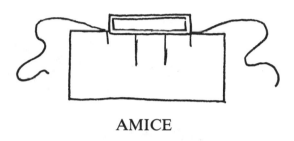

AMICE

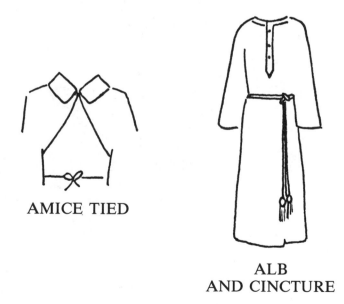

AMICE TIED

ALB
AND CINCTURE

c.   The cassock-alb is a single garment incorporating the amice and alb. Again, it is of such length as to come to the top of the shoes. The cassock-alb is worn with or without a cincture. However, the cincture is desirable for holding the garment properly in place and taking up any extra length.

**CASSOCK-ALB
AND CINCTURE**

d. On festive occasions, the crucifer may be vested in a tunic. This colored, sleeved vestment is worn over the cassock-alb (or alb and amice) and cincture—not over a cassock and surplice. It may either match the vestments of the ministers or be of a different color.

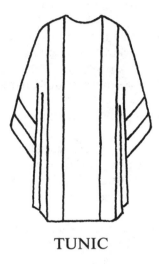

TUNIC

e. It is not advisable that the thurifer be vested in a tunic. The sleeves of this garment are easily caught in the chains or in the thurible itself! For safety and ease of movement either the cassock-alb or cassock and surplice are better.

Neatness is always in order: combed hair, polished shoes (preferably not sneakers or running shoes!), and clean hands and fingernails. Remember, your appearance should not distract the congregation.

Always be vested at least fifteen minutes before the service is to begin. This will leave you time for last minute preparations and instructions.

Chapter 5

The Lighting of Candles

The traditional manner for lighting the candles is as follows:

1. Always be vested before lighting the candles.
    They should be lighted ten minutes before the service.

2. Make sure the taper in the candle lighter is long enough.

3. Bend the taper slightly in case the wick of a candle is down.

4. Light the taper in the sacristy, before you go to the altar. (During the Fifty Days of Easter, the taper should be lighted from the Paschal Candle. If this candle is not already burning, it is always lighted first.)

5. Reverence the altar at the center. Then proceed to light the candles on the altar before any others.

    a. If there are two candles on the altar, the one on your right as you face the altar is lighted first. Bow again at the center and light the one on the left.

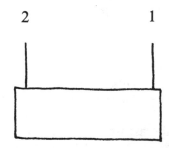

2   1

b. If there are six or more candles on the altar, start with the one on your right nearest the center and continue with the others, going to your right. Go back to the center, bow, start with the one on your left nearest the center, then light the others, going to your left.

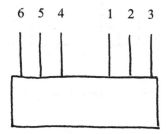

c. Other candles in the church should be lighted accordingly. (In some places the tradition is observed that at the main Eucharist on Sundays or feast days, all the candles on chapel or side altars are lighted.)

6. After you have finished lighting all of the candles, pull the lever on the pole to extinguish the taper and then immediately push it up again so that part of the taper is visible. This is done so that the wax on the taper does not melt inside and clog the tube.

7. Reverence the altar at the center and return to the sacristy.

8. On certain occasions, such as the Great Vigil of Easter or when the Order of Worship of the Evening is used, the candles are not lighted before the service but during it. Check with the celebrant before lighting candles on special days.

9.   If two people are assigned to light the candles, the procedure basically is the same. However, after reverencing the altar together, they light the candles nearest the center first (each taking a different side) and work outward. This should be done in a dignified and quiet way.

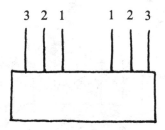

10.   In some places a wreath of fresh greens with four candles may hang in the chancel or some other place during the weeks of Advent. The candles are lighted as the weeks progress: one on the first Sunday, two on the second Sunday, and so on until all four candles burn on the Fourth Sunday of Advent. It is traditional to light those candles first.

Chapter 6

The Extinguishing of Candles

After the celebrant finishes the prayer in the sacristy the candles are extinguished.

1. Take the candle lighter, go to the center of the altar and reverence. The candles are extinguished in the reverse order from the way they were lighted. Those on the main altar should be extinguished first.

    a. If there are two candles, the one on your left as you face the altar is extinguished first. Go to the center, bow, and extinguish the other.

    b. If there are six or more candles on the altar, start with the one on the left farthest from the center and work toward the center. Then bow, and start with the one on the right farthest from the center and work toward the center.

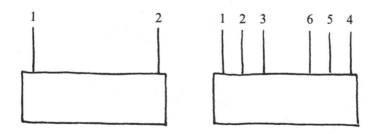

    c.   All other candles are extinguished after those on the main altar.

    d.   During the Fifty Days of Easter, if the Paschal Candle does not burn at all times, it should be extinguished last.

    e.   During Advent, it is traditional to extinguish the candles on the Advent Wreath last.

2.   After all of the candles (except the Sacrament lamp) have been extinguished, come back to the center, reverence the altar, and return to the sacristy. Put the candle lighter in its place and remove your vestments.

3.   If two servers are assigned to extinguish the candles, the procedure is the same. After reverencing the altar together, begin with the candles on either end, farthest from the center, and work towards the center. After the altar candles have been extinguished, other candles are extinguished (remember, the Paschal Candle is last during Eastertide!). The servers come to the center, reverence the altar and return to the sacristy.

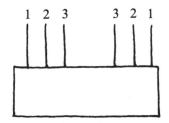

4. Important notes on extinguishing candles:

    a. Be sure to check the inside of the extinguisher, making sure that there is no residue of wax. If there is, clean it out before extinguishing the candles. Old wax can easily melt and create a messy blotch of wax and soot falling on altar linens or vestments.

    b. When extinguishing candles, the purpose is not to drown them in their own wax, but rather to cut off the oxygen. Therefore, do not plunge the extinguisher down over the top of the candle, but rather hold it gently over the flame until the candle is out.

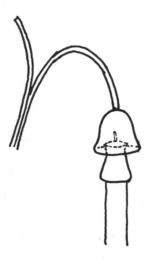

    c. After extinguishing each candle turn the snuffer up. This will keep melted wax from spilling on the altar linen.

    d. If for some reason you must blow the candles out rather than using an extinguisher, be careful. Place your hand behind the flame—otherwise wax will fly all over the place!

Chapter 7

Before the Eucharist

Arrive at least twenty minutes before the service begins. Vest immediately; then ask for any instructions from the celebrant or person in charge. After you are vested, it is a good idea to check the credence.

1. If the gifts are not being presented by members of the congregation, the following should be on the credence:
    a. Chalice, purificator, paten, bread or host, pall, corporal. If the above are covered with a veil, the burse is placed on top and contains the corporal and an extra purificator. In some places, especially at weekday celebrations, the celebrant will carry these in at the entrance.

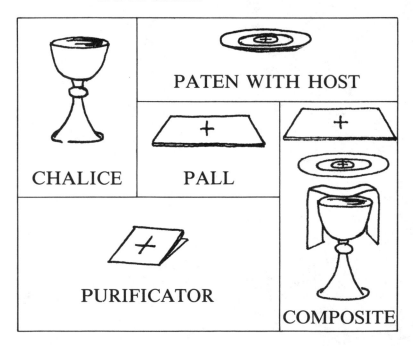

PATEN WITH HOST

CHALICE   PALL

PURIFICATOR

COMPOSITE

BURSE   **CORPORAL**

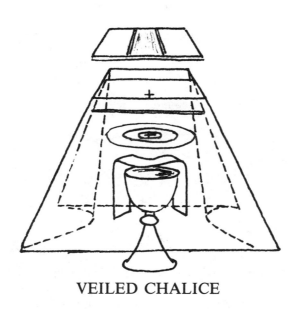

VEILED CHALICE

b. Bread box with wafers or bread.

c. A cruet of wine and a cruet of water.

BREAD BOX   CRUET

d. Lavabo bowl and towel.

LAVABO BOWL
AND TOWEL

e. A second chalice and purificator, if needed.

f. An extra cruet or flagon with wine, if necessary.

2. If the gifts are being presented by members of the congregation be sure that the lavabo bowl and towel (and anything else they may not bring up—see above list) are on the credence.

Ten minutes before the service light the candles (*see* Chapter 5). Be ready, quiet, and prepared for the start of the service. If you are carrying a candle, light it; if you are thurifer, make sure your coals are very hot; if you are crucifer, have your cross in hand.

Loud talking, or anything that might distract the congregation, is always out of order.

Part Two
The Holy Eucharist

Chapter 8
An Outline of the Eucharist

The Holy Eucharist

The Word of God

The Entrance	[Hymn, psalm, or anthem] [A Penitential Order]
The Preparation	Acclamation [Collect for Purity] [Summary of the Law] Song(s) of Praise
The Collect of the Day	
The Lessons	Lesson (Old Testament, Acts, Revelation, Apocrypha) [Psalm] Epistle (Letters of New Testament, Acts, or Revelation) [Alleluia (or Tract)] [Sequence Hymn] Gospel

The Sermon

The Nicene Creed

The Prayers of the People

Confession of Sin

[Comfortable Words]

The Peace

The Holy Communion

The Offertory	Sentence of Scripture, hymn, psalm, or anthem Presentation and preparation of the gifts [Lavabo]
The Great Thanksgiving	Salutation and Preface Sanctus Consecration [(Memorial) Acclamation] Doxology Lord's Prayer
The Breaking of the Bread	Anthem [Agnus Dei] [Prayer of Humble Access] Invitation to Communion Ministration of Communion [Hymn, psalm, or anthem] [Ablutions] Post-communion prayer of thanksgiving [Hymn] [Blessing] Dismissal [Hymn]

Chapter 9

Basic Instructions and Duties
of the Server at the Eucharist

The Holy Eucharist	The Holy Eucharist
When the Celebrant is behind the Altar, facing the People	When the Celebrant faces the Cross with back to Congregation

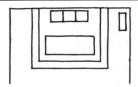   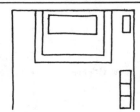

## The Word of God	## The Word of God
(page 323 or 355)	*(page 323 or 355)*
The Entrance	**The Entrance**
After a prayer of preparation, the S leads the C into the sanctuary.	After a prayer of preparation, the S leads the C into the sanctuary.
They reverence the altar together. *(Fig. 1)*	They reverence the altar together. *(Fig. 2)*
The Preparation, Hymn of Praise, and Collect of the Day (323-25 or 355-57)	**The Preparation, Hymn of Praise, and Collect of the Day** (323-25 or 355-57)
The C and S remain facing the altar until the conclusion of the Collect of the Day. S makes response and says or sings the Hymn of Praise.	S stands at the foot of the steps, to the left of C facing the altar. S makes response and says or sings the Hymn of Praise.
or	*or*
The C and S go directly to the sedilia. S remains standing at C's left. *(Fig. 3)*	The C and S go directly to the sedilia. S remains standing at C's left. *(Fig. 4)*
or	*or*
S goes to appointed place.	S goes to appointed place.

Notes: S = Server (or Acolyte)

C = Celebrant

Page numbers refer to *The Book of Common Prayer* (Rite I *or* Rite II)

Illustrations	The Holy Eucharist
	Optional Variants

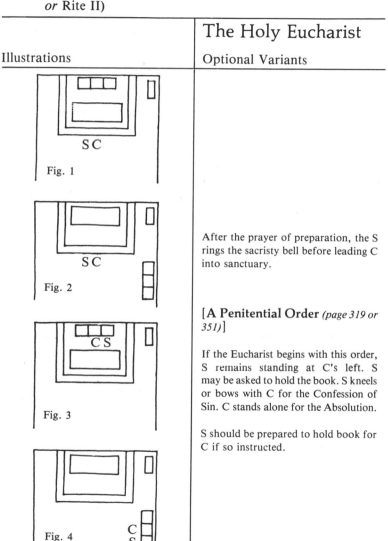

Fig. 1

Fig. 2

After the prayer of preparation, the S rings the sacristy bell before leading C into sanctuary.

Fig. 3

[A Penitential Order *(page 319 or 351)*]

If the Eucharist begins with this order, S remains standing at C's left. S may be asked to hold the book. S kneels or bows with C for the Confession of Sin. C stands alone for the Absolution.

S should be prepared to hold book for C if so instructed.

Fig. 4

Facing the People	Facing the Cross
The Lessons *(325 or 357)*	**The Lessons** *(325 or 357)*
S sits at the sedilia or other assigned place while C or other person reads the lesson and/or epistle.	S remains standing in place at the foot of the steps, or if convenient sits at the sedilia or some other assigned place, while C or other person reads the lesson and/or epistle.
S makes the responses at the conclusion of the readings.	S makes the responses at the conclusion of the readings.
S reads the psalm (alleluia verse or tract) with C.	S reads the psalm (alleluia verse or tract) with C.
S stands facing the reader for the proclamation of the Gospel and makes the responses *(326 or 357)*.	S stands facing the reader for the proclamation of the Gospel and makes the responses *(326 or 357)*.
The Sermon *(326 or 358)*	**The Sermon** *(326 or 358)*
S sits for the sermon.	S sits for the sermon.
The Nicene Creed	**The Nicene Creed**
S stands for the Creed and recites with C.	S stands for the Creed and recites with C.
The Prayers of the People *(328-30 or 359, 383 ff.)*	**The Prayers of the People** *(328-30, or 359, 383 ff.)*
S remains standing at sedilia and makes responses.	S remains standing at sedilia or at the foot of the altar steps and makes responses.

Illustrations	Optional Variants
	If instructed by C, S may read the lesson and/or epistle either from the lectern or in place.
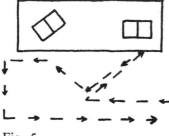 Fig. 5	If the collect, lesson, and epistle have been read from the right side of the altar, S may be instructed to move the Altar Book to the left side after the epistle [psalm, alleluia verse, or tract]. S goes to the center, reverences the altar, goes to C's right, picks up the book (and stand). S then goes back to center, bows, and places book on the left side of the altar. S then returns to place at the foot of the steps on the right side of the altar, facing C. *(Fig. 5)* S may be instructed to hold the Gospel Book for the reader.
	S may be instructed to lead the Prayers of the People. C *always* reads the concluding collect (or absolution if Form VI is used).

Facing the People	Facing the Cross
Confession of Sin *(330 or 360)*	**Confession of Sin** *(330 or 360)*
After the Invitation, S either bows or kneels depending on the posture of C.	After the Invitation, S either bows or kneels depending on the posture of C.
S says the Confession with C.	S says the Confession with C.
C stands alone for the Absolution. S remains bowing or kneeling [also for the Comfortable Words].	C stands alone for the Absolution. S remains bowing or kneeling [also for the Comfortable Words].
The Peace *(332 or 360)*	**The Peace** *(332 or 360)*
S stands and exchanges the Peace with C, according to the custom of the parish.	S stands and exchanges the Peace with C, according to the custom of the parish.

The Holy Communion *(333 or 361)*	The Holy Communion *(333 or 361)*
The Offertory	**The Offertory**
(After the Offertory Sentence) S goes to credence for presentation of gifts:	(After the Offertory Sentence) S goes to credence for presentation of gifts:
1. S brings (veiled) chalice, paten, (burse) corporal to C at altar.	1. S brings (veiled) chalice, paten, (burse) corporal to C at altar.
2. S brings bread box (indicating how many people are present) to C. C returns box to S. S puts box on credence. *(Fig. 6)*	2. S brings bread box (indicating how many people are present) to C. C returns box to S. S puts box on credence. *(Fig. 6)*
3. S brings wine (V) and water (A) cruets to C. These should be opened and held in the palm of the hand, with the handles facing the C—wine in right hand, water in left. *(Fig. 7)*	3. S brings wine (V) and water (A) cruets to C. These should be opened and held in the palm of the hand, with the handles facing the C—wine in right hand, water in left. *(Fig. 7)*

Illustrations	Optional Variants
	If the Penitential Order was used at the beginning of the Eucharist, the Confession is omitted here. If a confession of sin was part of the Prayers of the People (Forms I, V, or VI), it is omitted here.
	S may be instructed to go with C to the congregation and greet them with the Peace, according to the custom of the parish.
 Fig. 6	If the gifts are brought to the altar by members of the congregation, S stands with C in front of the altar. C (or deacon) receives the gifts and prepares them. S takes bread box, cruets, alms basin to credence after C is finished. S may have to bring (veiled) chalice, paten, (burse) corporal from credence to C if these are not brought up by members of the congregation. When receiving or returning gifts, or after lavabo, C may acknowledge S with a simple bow. If so, S bows to C.
 Fig. 7	If S receives the alms basin from representatives of the congregation, this is done *after* presenting bread, wine, and water to C. After it is offered it should be returned to credence. (In some places it is left on the altar.)

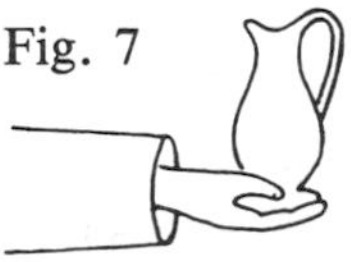

Facing the People	Facing the Cross
4. C takes wine, returns it, then takes water. (S presents with right hand and receives with left.) After C has finished with water, S returns cruets to credence. *(Fig. 8)*	4. C takes wine, returns it, then takes water. (S presents with right hand and receives with left.) After C has finished with water, S returns cruets to credence. *(Fig. 8)*
[Lavabo]	[Lavabo]
5. S then washes C's hands. S places towel over left arm, takes bowl in left hand and opened water cruet in right hand (by the handle). S pours water over C's fingers, then turns slightly to present towel. When C is finished, towel is returned to S's arm and S goes to credence to replace vessels. *(Fig. 9)*	5. S then washes C's hands. S places towel over left arm, takes bowl in left hand and opened water cruet in right hand (by the handle). S pours water over C's fingers, then turns slightly to present towel. When C is finished, towel is returned to S's arm and S goes to credence to replace vessels. *(Fig. 9)*
6. If the Altar Book (and stand) are not already on the altar, S brings them now and places them at C's left.	6. If the Altar Book (and stand) are not already on the altar, S brings them now and places them at C's left.
The Great Thanksgiving *(333-36, 340 ff. or 361-64, 367 ff.)*	**The Great Thanksgiving** *(333-36, 340 ff. or 361-64, 367 ff.)*
S stands at the right end of the altar or at other appointed place facing C.	S stands on the floor at right corner of steps facing the altar or at other appointed place.
S makes responses to salutation and preface.	S makes responses to salutation and preface.
S bows with C for the Sanctus.	S bows with C for the Sanctus.
S remains standing after Sanctus or kneels according to the custom of the parish.	S remains standing after Sanctus or kneels according to the custom of the parish.
[S says memorial acclamation as directed.]	[S says memorial acclamation as directed.]
S responds with Amen at end of Doxology.	S responds with Amen at end of Doxology.
S recites the Lord's Prayer with C.	S recites the Lord's Prayer with C.

Illustrations	Optional Variants

Fig. 8

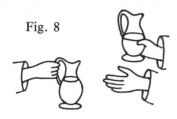

Fig. 9

S may be instructed to close the communion rail gates at this point.

S rings Sanctus bell three times at the words "Holy, Holy, Holy."

S rings bell at each of the elevations if directed by C.

S rings bell at concluding elevation if directed by C.

Facing the People	Facing the Cross
The Breaking of the Bread *(337 or 364)*	**The Breaking of the Bread** *(337 or 364)*
S responds to the Anthem at the Breaking of the Bread.	S responds to the Anthem at the Breaking of the Bread.
[S says Agnus Dei or other Anthem with C.]	[S says Agnus Dei or other Anthem with C.]
[S may say the Prayer of Humble Access with C.]	[S may say the Prayer of Humble Access with C.]
S receives Communion either standing or kneeling, according to the custom of the parish.	S receives Communion either standing or kneeling, according to the custom of the parish.
S remains in place, returns to sedilia, or stands/kneels near the credence.	S remains in place, returns to sedilia, or stands/kneels near the credence.
[Ablutions]	**[Ablutions]**
When C returns to altar, S, after reverencing the altar, goes to the credence and brings wine and water cruets. S holds cruets, opened, by the handles—wine in right hand, water in left.	When C returns to altar, S, after reverencing the altar, goes to the credence and brings wine and water cruets. S holds cruets, opened, by the handles—wine in right hand, water in left.
1. S first pours a little wine into the chalice. *(Fig. 10)*	1. S first pours a little wine into the chalice. *(Fig. 10)*
2. When C presents chalice with fingers over it, S first pours a little wine, then water over them. *(Fig. 11)*	2. When C presents chalice with fingers over it, S first pours a little wine, then water over them. *(Fig. 11)*

Illustrations	Optional Variants
	If there is a second chalice, S brings it from credence to altar.
	If the communion rail gates have not been closed earlier, S reverences the altar, then closes the gates and returns to place.
	If S is licensed by the Bishop to administer the chalice, S may assist C in the administration of Communion, as instructed.
 Fig. 10	C may do the ablutions at the credence table rather than at the altar.
	C may instruct water only for the ablutions.
 Fig. 11	The ablutions may be done by a deacon or assisting minister, either at the altar or at the credence.

Facing the People	Facing the Cross
S returns cruets to credence, replaces the covers. C may give chalice and paten to S to replace on credence table.	S returns cruets to credence, replaces the covers. C may give chalice and paten to S to replace on credence table.
S opens the gates of the communion rail, then returns to place and either stands or kneels.	S opens the gates of the communion rail, then returns to right corner of the steps facing the altar and either stands or kneels.
Thanksgiving, [Blessing], and Dismissal *(339 or 365)*	**Thanksgiving, [Blessing], and Dismissal** *(339 or 365)*
S remains standing or kneeling for the prayer of Thanksgiving. S may recite prayer with C.	S remains standing or kneeling for the prayer of Thanksgiving. S may recite prayer with C.
[S kneels or remains standing for Blessing.]	[S kneels or remains standing for Blessing.]
S stands for the Dismissal and makes the response "Thanks be to God."	S stands for the Dismissal and makes the response "Thanks be to God."
S comes to center with C and together they reverence the altar.	S comes to center with C and together they reverence the altar.
S leads C back into sacristy.	S leads C back into sacristy.
After prayers, S extinguishes the candles (*see* Chapter 6).	After prayers, S extinguishes the candles (*see* Chapter 6).

Part Three
Specific Duties at the Eucharist

Chapter 10
When There Is More Than One Server

If more than one person is assigned to serve at the Eucharist, the general duties described in Chapter 9 are the same. However, the responsibilities may be divided as follows:

1. If there are two servers, walk as a pair (carrying torches or candles, *see* Chapter 11). Walk ahead of the celebrant (and other assisting ministers) and, if incense is used, walk behind the thurifer.

2. If there are three servers, one should be crucifer (*see* Chapter 12) and the other two servers/acolytes. The servers walk with the crucifer, on either side. If incense is used, walk behind the thurifer.

3. If there are no other assisting ministers (concelebrants, deacon, subdeacon, lay readers) the servers should stand at either side of the altar, or together on the side of the sanctuary nearest the credence table.

4. If the servers sit with the celebrant at the sedilia, one should be on either side of the celebrant.

5. Servers may be asked by the celebrant to read the lesson, the epistle, or lead the prayers of the people.

6. At the Offertory:

    a. one server should present the bread box and the

other the cruets.

b. only one server should wash the hands of the celebrant —the other may receive the alms, and after presenting them to the celebrant, return them to the credence. The servers should close the gates of the communion rail.

7. If licensed by the Bishop, servers may assist with the ministration of Communion.

8. At the end, the servers lead the celebrant back to the sacristy either walking as a pair or with the crucifer, carrying lighted torches.

Chapter 11

The Acolyte

The acolyte, torchbearer, or candlebearer is a server who carries a candle or a torch. These are always carried in pairs, never singly. If there is a crucifer, the acolytes walk with lighted candles on either side in line with the crucifer.

SOME GENERAL PRINCIPLES

1. Carry the candle so that it is even with the other acolyte's candle. Ideally the light should be level with your forehead, however, if your partner is of a different height, adjustment should be made. The main point is that the candles when carried are at an equal height.

2. There are two types of torches:

   a. One on a long pole without a stand *(type a)*.

   b. The other a shorter candle with a base *(type b)*.

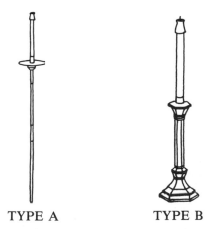

TYPE A   TYPE B

3. Carrying the torches:

type a. Grasp the pole firmly with both hands in such a way that the torch will be balanced and you will not tip it and drop wax all over the place, or on yourself! Be careful of stairs. Remember to raise the pole slightly, so that it doesn't catch on a step. When standing still and holding a torch, you may rest it on the floor to keep it balanced.

type b. One hand should be around the neck of the holder and the other supporting the base. This will ensure a steady grasp.

4. *Never bow or genuflect when holding a torch or candle.* Always be reverent and dignified, but be careful of spilling wax!

5. Always carry a package of matches with you in case a candle should go out during the service. If it does go out, light it discreetly and don't make a fuss.

6. The Acolytes will usually be the servers at the Eucharist. Follow the instructions in Chapter 9 for the basic directions, but add the following:

AT THE ENTRANCE

Walk with the crucifer, stop briefly in front of the altar and then place your candles in their holders (if *type a*) or on the credence table or some other appropriate place (if *type b*). They should remain lighted throughout the service. Extinguishing and lighting candles again is only distracting!

AT A SOLEMN PROCESSION

Carrying lighted candles, walk on either side of the crucifer.

AT THE GOSPEL

During the alleluia, tract, or sequence hymn take your candle and prepare for the Gospel procession. When the reader of the Gospel goes to the altar, come from your place and stand either at the foot of the steps or on either side of the reader. Walk with the reader to the place of the proclamation of the Gospel. (You might be instructed to walk either with the crucifer or ahead of the reader. If there is incense, always walk behind the thurifer.) When you reach the place where the Gospel is proclaimed, stand on either side of the book facing your partner. If *type a* torches are used, rest them on the floor. If *type b* torches are used, hold them at the same level.

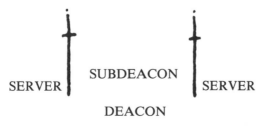

SUBDEACON

SERVER   SERVER

DEACON

AT THE GOSPEL

After the Gospel is proclaimed, either walk with the reader, or ahead of the reader back to the altar, pause, and replace your candles either in their holders or on the credence table, or other appropriate place. Go to your place and sit during the sermon.

AT THE RETIRING PROCESSION

After the dismissal (or closing hymn) take your candles and as soon as the crucifer is in place, go and stand on either side of the crucifer facing the altar. When ready (walking with the crucifer) lead the procession back to the sacristy. If there is a thurifer, the acolytes always follow, walking as a pair or with the crucifer.

Note: In some places it is customary for the acolytes to take their candles at the beginning of the Great Thanksgiving and stand or kneel in front of the altar. If this is the case, take the torches or candles, come to the center (do not bow or genuflect), and then go to the sides and remain there standing or kneeling as directed until the conclusion of the Lord's Prayer.

Chapter 12

The Crucifer

The primary function of the crucifer is to carry the processional cross at the entrance, during a solemn procession, at the gospel procession, and at the retiring procession. The crucifer may also be expected to do some of the other assisting actions which are general responsibilities of the servers (*see* Chapter 9).

SOME GENERAL PRINCIPLES

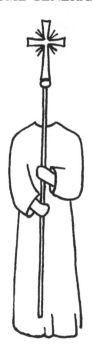

1. The cross must always be carried with dignity. Any position that would look either stiff or sloppy must be avoided. The best way is to hold it firmly with both hands in the middle of the pole. Your elbows should be relaxed. Be sure that the symbol or figure of Christ crucified is facing out. Carry the processional cross slightly raised from the ground. This all depends on your height—but in all cases make sure that it is held firmly and that the position looks relaxed and dignified.

2. The crucifer leads the procession at the entrance (unless incense is used, in which case the crucifer follows at least six feet behind the thurifer). The cross is placed in its holder and secured. The crucifer goes to the place assigned.

3. When carrying the processional cross, never bow or genuflect.

4. Be careful of steps. Raise the pole slightly higher when approaching them. Also, be careful of low beams, hanging advent wreaths, "invisible" electrical wires, or the like. Lower the cross whenever there is a chance that you may hit these objects.

5. Carry the cross straight, not tilting forward or backward. This takes practice and be sure you know what you are doing before you have to do it!

AT THE ENTRANCE

After the prayer of preparation in the sacristy, lead the procession to the altar, walking slowly and with dignity. If there are torch-bearers they should be on either side of you. Pause in front of the altar (do not bow!) then place the cross in its holder. If you have to pass in front of the altar to get to your place, reverence the altar when doing so.

AT A SOLEMN PROCESSION (*see also* Chapter 17)

Proceed in as at the entrance, but do not put the cross in its holder. Stand in a convenient place, with the acolytes, holding the cross. If incense is used, the crucifer follows the thurifer around the church. If there is no thurifer, the crucifer, with the acolytes on either side, leads the procession. If a station is made, the thurifer may stop at the place so that the celebrant may fill the thurible. The crucifer should continue on until the celebrant is at the place of the station, then stop, turn, and face the celebrant. After the collect, wait until the thurifer is again in front of you and then follow. If there is no thurifer, begin walking again after the stational collect. When the procession returns to the sanctuary, put the cross in its holder and go to your place.

AT THE GOSPEL (optional)

In some places it is customary to have the crucifer lead the Gospel procession. During the alleluia, tract, or sequence hymn, get the cross and take it to some convenient place. Do not stand in front of the altar, since the reader will have to get the Gospel book. When the reader turns from the altar with the book, lead the procession to the place from which the Gospel is proclaimed. (The crucifer follows the thurifer if incense is used.) At the place of the proclamation the crucifer turns and faces the reader, standing behind the sub deacon or other person holding the book. The torches should be on either side of the book, not on either side of the crucifer. Rest the base of the cross on the floor during the proclamation of the Gospel.

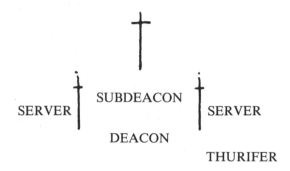

AT THE GOSPEL

At the conclusion, rather than trying to get around the people in front of you, simply follow the procession back to the altar, put the cross in its place, and go to your place.

AT THE RETIRING PROCESSION

After the dismissal, get the cross, return to the center and wait for the acolytes to arrive on either side of you with their torches. Then lead the procession back to the sacristy. Again, if the thurifer carries the thurible, follow behind.

Note: In some places the retiring procession does not move until the concluding hymn is finished.

Chapter 13

The Thurifer

The thurifer is one who carries the thurible and boat when incense is used at the Eucharist or other celebrations. The traditional use of incense at the Eucharist is at the entrance, during a solemn procession, at the Gospel, and at the Offertory. In some places incense is used for blessings and other indications of honor or reverence. The responsibilities of the thurifer are important and must be carried out carefully and reverently. Remember, this is not a show, and the focus of attention should not be on the thurifer.

SOME GENERAL PRINCIPLES

1. Always have both the thurible and the boat—don't ever forget the boat!

   a. The thurible should be held at the top of the chain, not by the ring, if there is only one chain *(type a)*.

TYPE A

b. If there is more than one chain *(type b)*, hold the thurible securely under the disc in such a way that you will not burn yourself or drop it.

TYPE B

The thurible is held in the right hand, the boat in the left.

2. Make sure there is incense and a spoon in the boat.

3. At least ten minutes before the celebration begins, the charcoal should be lighted. Use a pair of tongs to hold the piece of charcoal and then carefully light it. Once you are sure that it is lighted, place it in the thurible and light another piece in the same way. Ideally, there should be three pieces of charcoal (or more, if a large thurible is used) in the thurible.

4. Always make sure that the coals are hot. You may have to use new ones before the Gospel if there has been a solemn procession at the entrance. Always put new coals in for the Offertory. Again, give them enough time to be very hot— about ten minutes before they will be required. Discard the old ones in a safe container before putting fresh charcoal in the thurible.

5. The procedure for presenting the incense to fill the thurible is as follows:

    a. Go to the celebrant and stand facing the celebrant. (If a bishop is present, kneel if the bishop is sitting.)

    b. Hand the boat to the deacon or some other assisting minister, or to the celebrant if there is no assisting minister.

    c. Raise the lid of the thurible, either by sliding the top of the thurible up the chains, or pulling the chain with the ring on the end.

    d. Never touch the bottom of the thurible or you will risk the chance of a bad burn!

    e. Using your left hand, raise the thurible by the chains to a level easy for the celebrant to fill it. The celebrant will then put the incense on the coals (and bless it). The thurifer then carefully closes the lid, takes a firm grasp of the chains *(see above)* and takes the boat back from the deacon (or person holding it) and holds it in the left hand.

    f. Again, don't touch the thurible itself; it is very hot!

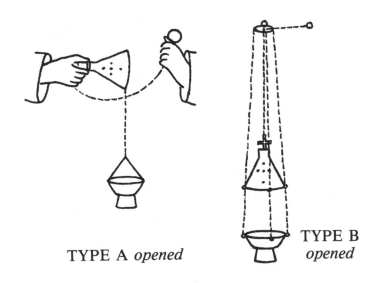

TYPE A *opened*

TYPE B *opened*

AT THE ENTRANCE

The celebrant may fill the thurible with incense before the entrance, or may instruct the thurifer to do so. After the prayers in the sacristy, the thurifer leads the procession to the altar. The thurifer walks in front of the crucifer and acolytes, unless there are several processions, in which case the thurifer walks in front of the acolytes preceding the celebrant and assisting ministers. The thurible is swung gently when walking.

Bring the thurible and boat to the celebrant (or bishop). The thurible is filled. The celebrant will then cense the altar either during the Introit, or opening hymn, or during the Hymn of Praise. The celebrant will then return the thurible to the thurifer. Stay in place until the conclusion of the Collect of the Day (or immediately return to the sacristy).

AT A SOLEMN PROCESSION

The entrance is usually made in the same way as above. However, after the celebrant fills the thurible (and blesses the incense), the thurifer keeps the thurible and prepares for the procession.

After the deacon (or person appointed) sings "Let us go forth in peace," the thurifer leads the procession around the church (*see* Chapter 17). The celebrant may instruct you that there will be a station, at which time the thurible may be filled with incense again. Remember, walk slowly and swing the thurible in a dignified way. Also, remember the boat!

When the procession returns to the altar, follow the procedure above for the filling of the thurible and censing of the altar.

AT THE GOSPEL

As soon as the alleluia, tract, or sequence hymn begins, come from the sacristy, reverence the altar and go to the celebrant (or bishop). Present for filling (and blessing) in the usual way, then take the thurible and boat. Stand ready for the Gospel. After the reader has taken the Gospel book from the altar (and received the bishop's blessing), lead the procession to the place from which the Gospel is to be proclaimed. (After the reader announces the Gospel, hand the thurible, again by the chains, so that the deacon or reader may cense the Gospel book.) Remain standing at the reader's right until the conclusion of the proclamation of the Gospel. Then lead the procession back into the sanctuary, reverence the altar, and go to the sacristy.

Remember, you will probably need fresh coals at this point.

AT THE OFFERTORY

The thurifer may either lead the Offertory Procession up to the altar, or come to the altar directly from the sacristy, depending on the custom of the parish. If you come from the sacristy, be sure you are near the altar and not in the way. Remember to take the boat! Stay in a convenient place until the gifts have been presented and offered. Then go to the celebrant, and present the thurible to be filled (and blessed) in the usual way. The boat will be returned to you and the celebrant will take the thurible. Then, get out of the way, while the celebrant censes the gifts and the altar. When finished, the celebrant will either give the thurible to you or to the deacon or other assisting minister.

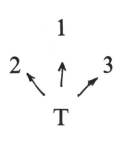

a. If the celebrant gives it to the deacon, the deacon will cense the celebrant, (bishop), and then give it to you. You then cense those in the sanctuary (either as a group or individually) and then the congregation. When censing a group of people, bow to them first, then one swing to the center, one swing to the left, one swing to the right. Bow again and return to your place.

b. If the celebrant gives the thurible directly to you, go to the center of the sanctuary and cense all those there in the way described above and then turn and cense the people.

c. In some places, the celebrant censes the gifts and altar only, and those in the sanctuary or the congregation are not censed.

Note: The above is subject to parish custom and use—in other words, do whatever you are instructed.

After this is finished return to your place in the sanctuary (or return to the sacristy if so instructed). If you remain in the sanctuary, it is traditional to swing the thurible (three times) at the Sanctus; (three times) at each of the elevations; and (three times) at the elevation during the doxology at the end of the Great Thanksgiving.

The thurifer then returns to the sacristy, either after the Lord's Prayer or after the Breaking of the Bread. Put the thurible in a safe place, discard the coals, and make sure that there is no chance of fire!

AT THE RETIRING PROCESSION

If you are instructed by the celebrant to lead the procession out of the church with incense, either:

a. fill the thurible with incense yourself before you come into the sanctuary.

b. or go to the celebrant (or bishop) to fill it in the usual way.

After the dismissal (or closing hymn) lead the procession out, again swinging the thurible gently.

If incense is not used in the retiring procession, then walk immediately after the crucifer and acolytes, or simply stay in the sacristy.

Note: It is customary that the bishop, whether celebrating or presiding, fills the thurible and blesses incense.

Note: In some places, a person is designated to assist the thurifer by carrying the boat. Although this has its educational value in training someone to be thurifer, it also may cause considerable confusion and unnecessary fussiness during the service. The general consensus is that the thurifer should carry out the responsibilities alone, carrying both the thurible and boat.

Part Four

Other Liturgies

Chapter 14
The Daily Offices:
Morning or Evening Prayer
(BCP, pp. 37-126)

Light the candles as directed by the officiant.

1. If these offices are read simply, there is no need of a server, except possibly to read the lessons.

2. If these offices are used as the first part of the Eucharist (The Word of God) then the duties of the server are as described for the Eucharist (*see* Chapter 9). The difference, so far as the server is concerned, is that the office will be read from the chancel and a Gospel procession is not ordinarily used.

3. If these offices are used solemnly, the server may be required to do some of the following:

    a. At the entrance, incense, cross and torches may be used.

    b. Incense may be used during the Invitatory or during one of the Canticles.

    c. The acolytes may stand on either side of the officiant, holding their torches, for the prayers after the readings.

4. If Morning or Evening Prayer is used as a main service, there

might be an entrance with cross and candles. The server may be required to receive the money offering of the people and present it to the officiant. Cross and candles may be used at the retiring procession.

Extinguish the candles.

Chapter 15

An Order of Worship for the Evening

(BCP, pp. 108-14)

This Order may be used "as a complete rite in place of Evening Prayer, or as the introduction to Evening Prayer, the Eucharist, or at other times" *(p. 108)*.

1. The candles are not lighted before the service.

2. Torches (lighted) may be carried in front of the officiant, as well as the processional cross and incense. The purpose of the lighted torches is to provide light for the officiant to read.

3. The acolytes should stand with the officiant for the Opening Acclamation, the short Lesson of Scripture, and the Prayer for Light *(pp. 109-11)*.

4. After the Prayer for Light, the candles in the church and those of the congregation are lighted.

5. During the *Phos hilaron (p. 112),* or some other appropriate hymn, the officiant may cense the altar. Incense is presented and the thurible filled in the usual way.

6. The service continues with Evening Prayer, the Collect of the Day at the Eucharist, or some other office or devotion.

Chapter 16

Holy Baptism; Celebration and Blessing of a Marriage; Burial of the Dead

If these services are celebrated within the context of the Eucharist (for Baptism, this is the norm), the server(s) will have additional responsibilities. If celebrated apart from the Eucharist, the server's duties are directed by parish custom.

HOLY BAPTISM *(p. 299)*

The Baptismal rite itself takes place after the sermon (or after the Gospel). The servers may be asked to do the following:

1. Lead the procession to the font with cross and candles.

2. At the font, a server may be asked to

    a. hold the book for the celebrant during the thanksgiving over water *(p. 306)*, the baptism *(p. 307)*, the chrismation *(p. 308)*, and the prayers.

    b. hand the celebrant the pitcher with water to be poured into the font; the baptismal cup or shell, a towel, and the vessel with oil for the chrismation.

    c. wash the celebrant's hands after the chrismation or have a piece of cotton ready for cleansing the fingers.

    d. hand the celebrant a candle to be lighted from the Paschal candle *(p. 313)*.

3. Lead the Procession back to the altar with cross and candles.

CELEBRATION AND BLESSING OF A MARRIAGE *(p. 423)*

The server is to assist the celebrant as needed.

1. To carry the cross if it is used in the entrance procession.

2. If holy water is used for the blessing of the rings *(p. 427)* or at the nuptial blessing to present the aspergillum and bucket.

3. To hold the book when the celebrant is blessing the couple or performing other actions when the celebrant's hands need to be free.

BURIAL OF THE DEAD *(p. 469 or 491)*

The server may be required

1. To lead the procession into the church, carrying either the Paschal candle or the processional cross.

2. At the Commendation *(p. 482 or 499)*:

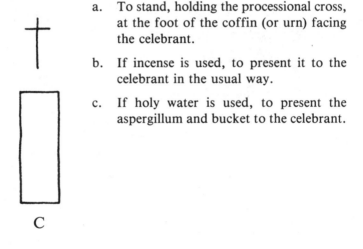

a. To stand, holding the processional cross, at the foot of the coffin (or urn) facing the celebrant.

b. If incense is used, to present it to the celebrant in the usual way.

c. If holy water is used, to present the aspergillum and bucket to the celebrant.

C

3. As the procession leaves the church, to lead carrying either the Paschal candle or the processional cross.

Chapter 17

Processions

A Procession is a formal walk around the church, or to a specific place, and is appropriate on Feast Days, Days of Special Prayer, or when the Great Litany is sung. The duties of the crucifer, acolytes and thurifer are as follows:

THE SOLEMN PROCESSION

A Solemn Procession is held prior to the Eucharist on Major Feast Days. The entrance is done in the usual way. If incense is used, it is prepared at the altar. The order for the procession is:

Thurifer

Acolyte   Crucifer   Acolyte

(Choir)

Assisting Ministers

(Subdeacon)

(Deacon)

Celebrant

(Bishop)

The route of the solemn procession may vary, but the normal procedure is that the procession begins and ends at the altar. After incense has been prepared and all are ready, the deacon (or celebrant) intones the bidding. After the response the thurifer (or if incense is not used, the crucifer and acolytes) leads the procession down the center aisle, turns right, across to the "north aisle," turns right, up the aisle, turns right, across the front (do not reverence the altar when passing in front) to the "south aisle," turns right, down the south aisle to the back, turns right to the center aisle, turns right and up the center aisle to the altar. A Station (that is, a stop for a versicle, response, and collect) at some appropriate place may be made during the procession. Incense may be used again at this point. The thurifer and crucifer should remember that the place of the station is where the celebrant should be; make sure that the procession is far enough ahead to ensure this. After the collect the thurifer leads the procession along the route back to the altar.

Route of the Solemn Procession

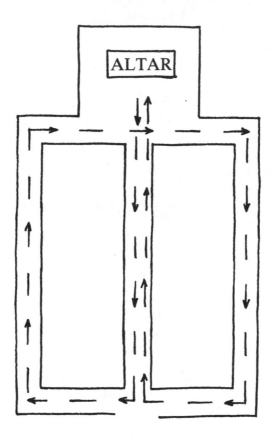

LITANY IN PROCESSION

On certain days, especially the Sundays of Advent and Lent, the Great Litany is sung in procession. The procession begins at the altar, but incense is not used. The procession remains facing the altar until after "O holy, blessed, and glorious Trinity, One God, have mercy upon us" *(p. 148)*. Then the crucifer and acolytes lead the procession around the church in the same pattern as the solemn procession. A station is not normally made. Walk slowly so that you return to the altar at just about the time the final petitions before the "Lamb of God" *(p. 152)* are concluded.

Note: During Lent, a lenten cross may be used in place of the usual processional cross.

THE ROGATION PROCESSION

On Rogation Sunday (the Sixth Sunday of Easter) or the days following, a procession may be made to bless the fields, crops, churchyard, garden, or, in a city, the neighborhood or block. This may either precede the Eucharist or follow it. The route of the procession will be determined by the priest, and a station or stations may be made. Even if the Great Litany is sung during this procession, it is appropriate to use incense, and thus the thurifer leads the procession.

SOME GENERAL POINTS TO REMEMBER ABOUT PROCESSIONS

Thurifer: Stay well ahead of the crucifer and swing the thurible gently. Any flamboyant or theatrical swings are out of place and only distracting. Also, make sure that you have enough hot coals in the thurible to last through the procession.

Crucifer: Keep your cross steady and firmly grasped. Don't let it lean forward, and remember to watch out for low hanging objects. It is a good idea to stay at least six feet behind the thurifer; otherwise you might get hit with the thurible!

Acolytes: Walk with the crucifer, or if the side aisles are narrow, as a pair behind the crucifer. Make sure that your torches or candles are of the same height and don't let them tilt and spill wax. Remember, watch out for stairs.

Servers: If other servers walk in the procession they should be in pairs, either holding a hymnal/prayer book or with hands folded above the waist. Don't walk with your hands swinging!

Everyone: Processions need to be carefully planned and rehearsed if you are not familiar with your parish use. Always check with the celebrant or person in charge as to the particulars of the procession.

Chapter 18
Proper Liturgies for Special Days

The Book of Common Prayer contains a number of liturgies for special occasions during the Church Year. The particular duties of the server/crucifer/acolyte/thurifer are briefly noted here. However, the precise ceremonial depends upon the use of the parish and the discretion of the priest.

ASH WEDNESDAY *(pp. 264-69)*

The entrance is done in the normal way. However, it may be done in silence without any musical accompaniment. Thurifer, crucifer and acolytes all perform their duties in the normal way.

After the Sermon an exhortation *(pp. 264-65)* is read and followed by the blessing of ashes. If the celebrant uses incense and/or holy water for this prayer, the thurifer and server should be prepared.

After the imposition of ashes, the server should wash the fingers of those who imposed the ashes, using water, lavabo bowl, and towel with the same procedure as at the Eucharist.

The Litany of Penitence *(p. 267)* follows and all kneel in place. The celebrant alone stands for the absolution *(p. 269)*. This is immediately followed by the Peace, and the Eucharist continues as usual with the Offertory.

THE SUNDAY OF THE PASSION: PALM SUNDAY *(pp. 270-73)*

The Liturgy of the Palms may be celebrated in a place apart from the church or in the chancel.

The entrance is made in the usual order, but goes to the place of the blessing of the palms rather than the altar. After the prayer, the deacon or other person reads the lesson *(p. 270)*. Candles or incense may be used at this Gospel lesson.

The blessing of the palms *(p. 271)* follows the reading. A server may be required to hold the book for the celebrant. If incense is used, the celebrant may wish to prepare the thurible before the blessing of palms and to cense the branches after the blessing. The thurifer should be prepared. (If the celebrant uses holy water for the blessing, a server should hold the aspergillum and bucket.)

The distribution of the palms may follow and servers be required to assist the celebrant.

The procession forms in the usual way (*see* Solemn Processions) and all carry palm branches (except crucifer, acolytes with torches, and thurifer). If the Liturgy of the Palms has taken place in some other location than the church, the procession now moves into the church. If all has been done in the church, the procession follows the usual route of a solemn procession. It is appropriate that a station be made at the door of the church *(pp. 271-72)*. The procession then proceeds to the altar.

The Eucharist begins with the Collect of the Day and all is as usual except that for the reading of the Passion (which is the Gospel for this day), torches or incense are not used.

MAUNDY THURSDAY *(pp. 274-75)*

The Eucharist as usual on this day, except:

1. If the washing of feet takes place after the sermon, the server may be required to assist the ministers in this ceremony.

2. If the Sacrament is to be reserved after communion, a server or servers may be required to go with the celebrant to the Place of Reservation, preceding the celebrant with candles (and incense).

3. At the end of the service, before the dismissal, the altars are stripped and other decorations are removed or covered. Servers may be instructed to assist in this. Also, the candles should be extinguished before the stripping of the altars begins.

Note: At the Place of Reservation for the Sacrament, the altar should not be stripped, nor should the candles be extinguished.

GOOD FRIDAY *(pp. 276-82)*

The entrance takes place in silence. Processional cross, torches, or incense are not used. The Passion Gospel is as on Palm Sunday, without the use of torches or incense. After the Solemn Collects *(p. 277)*, two acolytes may accompany the deacon or celebrant for the bringing in of the cross *(see p. 281)*. Lighted candles may be carried and placed with the cross either on the altar or some other appropriate place. If the people come forward for the Veneration of the Cross, the servers may be required to hold the cross.

If Communion is distributed from the Sacrament reserved from Maundy Thursday, the servers should be ready to assist with the bringing of necessary vessels and Altar Book from the credence to the altar (chalice, purificator, corporal). The deacon or celebrant brings the Sacrament from the Place of Reservation and places it (after the corporal has been laid) on the altar *(p. 282)*. (*Note*: In some places a full altar cloth is spread before the Sacrament is placed upon it. The servers may be asked to do this after the Veneration of the Cross is completed.)

After the prayer *(p. 282)*, all depart in silence (again without cross, candles, or incense).

HOLY SATURDAY

There is no celebration of the Eucharist *(p. 283)*. Servers—without incense, cross, or candles—assist as directed by the celebrant.

THE GREAT VIGIL OF EASTER *(pp. 284-295)*

The ceremonies for the Great Vigil may be quite complex. It is necessary for the servers to be well instructed and familiar with the rite. Again, the use is determined by each parish, but here are some of the general things of which servers should be aware.

1. The candles are not lighted before the service.

2. At the lighting of the Paschal Candle *(p. 285)*, the servers may be requested to assist the celebrant, and the thurifer should be prepared for incense to be used.

3. The procession into the church is lead by the deacon (or celebrant) carrying the Paschal Candle. The procession pauses three times for the proclamation "the Light of Christ." At each stop, candles are lighted (eg., those in the procession, then those of the congregation). If the acolytes are carrying torches they are lighted at the second stop in the procession. (*Note*: The altar candles are not lighted at this point.)

4. Before the singing of the Exsultet *(p. 286)*, the Paschal Candle may be censed. The thurifer should be prepared.

5. The servers sit in their places for the readings and stand for the collects *(p. 288)*.

6. If a procession is made to the Baptismal font, incense, cross, and torches may be carried. A server may be required to assist the celebrant as at a Baptism. The procession returns to the chancel, in the normal way. (The Great Litany may be sung at this point.)

7. The candles on the altar are lighted now *(p. 294)* and the Eucharist begins with the Easter Proclamation and a Hymn of Praise. Incense may be used here.

8. The rest of the Eucharist proceeds as usual, except that the Nicene Creed is omitted, and if the Great Litany has been used, the Prayers of the People are omitted.

9. The Paschal Candle is lighted for all services throughout the Fifty Days of Easter until the Day of Pentecost.

Appendix A

A Form for the Commissioning of Servers at the Altar

This form may be used following the homily (and Creed) at the Eucharist, or at the time of the hymn or anthem following the Collects in Morning or Evening Prayer, or separately.

Symbols appropriate to the ministry of servers may be given to the candidates as they are commissioned.

The Examination

The congregation being seated, the celebrant stands in full view of the people. The sponsors and candidates stand facing the celebrant.

The Celebrant says these or similar words

Brothers and Sisters in Christ Jesus, we are all baptized by the one Spirit into one Body, and given gifts for a variety of ministries for the common good. Our purpose is to commission *these persons* in the Name of God and of this congregation to a special ministry to which *they* are called.

The Celebrant asks the sponsor or sponsors

Are *these persons* you are to present prepared by a commitment to Christ as Lord, by regular attendance at worship, and by the knowledge of *their* duties, to exercise *their* ministry to the honor of God, and the well-being of his Church?

Sponsor   I believe *they are.*

The Celebrant then says these or similar words

You have been called to a ministry in this congregation. Will you as long as you are engaged in this work, perform it with diligence?

Candidate   I will.

Celebrant   Will you faithfully and reverently execute the duties of your ministry to the honor of God, and the benefit of the members of this congregation?

Candidate   I will.

When used as a separate service, a Scripture reading follows here.

The Commissioning

Sponsor   I present to you *these persons* to be admitted to the ministry of Server in this congregation.

Antiphon

Do not be negligent, for the Lord has chosen you to stand in his presence, to minister to him, and to be his minister.

V. I will go to the altar of God;
R. To the God of my joy and gladness.

Let us pray *(Silence)*

O God, our gracious Father: Bless the servers of your Church that they may so serve before your earthly altar in reverence and holiness, that they may attain, with all your saints and angels, the joy of serving you and worshiping you before your Heavenly Altar; through Jesus Christ our Lord. *Amen.*

In the Name of God and of this congregation, I commission you *N.* as Server in this *Parish*, (and give you this _____ as a token of your ministry).

When used with the Eucharist, the service continues with (the Prayers of the People and) the exchange of the Peace.

The following Collect may be used at the conclusion of the Prayers of the People

O Lord, without whom our labor is lost: We beseech you to prosper all works in your Church undertaken according to your holy will. Grant to your servers a pure intention, a patient faith, sufficient success on earth, and the blessedness of serving you in heaven; through Jesus Christ our Lord. *Amen.*

When used with the Daily Office, the service continues with the preceding prayer and the exchange of the Peace.

When used separately, it ends with the preceding prayer, the Lord's prayer, the exchange of the Peace, and a blessing.

The Church Year

Advent Season

The First Sunday of Advent

The Second Sunday of Advent

The Third Sunday of Advent

The Fourth Sunday of Advent

Christmas Season

The Nativity of Our Lord Jesus Christ:
  Christmas Day, *December 25*

The First Sunday after Christmas Day

The Holy Name of Our Lord Jesus Christ, *January 1*

The Second Sunday after Christmas Day

Epiphany Season

The Epiphany, or the Manifestation of Christ to the Gentiles,
  January 6

The First Sunday after the Epiphany:
  The Baptism of Our Lord Jesus Christ

The Second Sunday through the Eighth Sunday after the Epiphany

The Last Sunday after the Epiphany:
  (The Transfiguration of Our Lord Jesus Christ)

Lenten Season

The First Day of Lent, or Ash Wednesday

The First Sunday in Lent

The Second Sunday in Lent

The Third Sunday in Lent

The Fourth Sunday in Lent

The Fifth Sunday in Lent

Holy Week

The Sunday of the Passion: Palm Sunday

Monday in Holy Week

Tuesday in Holy Week

Wednesday in Holy Week

Maundy Thursday

Good Friday

Holy Saturday

Easter Season

Easter Eve: *(The Great Vigil of Easter)*

The Sunday of the Resurrection, or Easter Day

Monday through Saturday in Easter Week

The Second Sunday of Easter

The Third Sunday of Easter

The Fourth Sunday of Easter

The Fifth Sunday of Easter

The Sixth Sunday of Easter *(Rogation Sunday)*

Ascension Day *(40 days after Easter)*

The Seventh Sunday of Easter

The Day of Pentecost: Whitsunday

The Season After Pentecost

The First Sunday after Pentecost: Trinity Sunday

The Second Sunday through the Twenty-Seventh Sunday after Pentecost and All Saints' Day

The Last Sunday after Pentecost: *(Christ the King)*

For Holy Days see The Book of Common Prayer, 32-33.

For the Calendar of the Church Year see The Book of Common Prayer, 15-30.

Glossary of Terms

Ablutions   The cleansing of the chalice(s), paten, and other vessels after the administration of Communion. This may be done at the altar or at the credence, or after the dismissal.

Absolution   The pronouncement of God's forgiveness, after the Confession of Sin, by a bishop or priest at the Eucharist, Daily Offices, or in the Reconciliation of a Penitent *(BCP, 447ff.)*.

Acolyte   A term specifically applied to one who carries a torch or a candle in processions and at other times during the liturgy. This term is also commonly interchanged with server.

Acclamation   A versicle and response of praise at the beginning of the Eucharist and other services; also, in Rite II, the (memorial) response of the people during the Eucharistic Prayer.

Advent   The beginning of the Church Year (see *Appendix B*) and the four weeks leading up to and concluding with Christmas.

Advent Wreath   A circle of greens, with four candles, which hangs in the chancel or other place in the church during Advent. The candles are lighted consecutively week by week until all four are burning on the Fourth Sunday of Advent.

Agnus Dei   One of the anthems at the Breaking of the Bread; also found at the conclusion of the Great Litany *(BCP, 337, 407, 152)*.

Alb   A long, white, sleeved (linen) vestment worn over the cassock and amice (see *Chapter 4*).

Alleluia   An exclamation of praise and joy, used in various parts of the liturgy, except during Lent.

Alleluia Verse   A passage of scripture with the acclamation "alleluia" sung or said before the proclamation of the Gospel. The Alleluia Verse is not used in Lent (see *Tract*).

Alms Money or other offerings of the people for the work of the Church.

Alms Basin A large metal plate into which the money offerings of the people are placed before they are presented to the officiant.

Altar A stone or wooden table at which the Holy Eucharist is celebrated.

Altar Book The large book containing the texts from *The Book of Common Prayer* and music for the celebrant at the Eucharist and other liturgies.

Altar Cloth A long piece of white linen that covers the top of the altar and hangs down the sides almost to the floor. When not in use, the altar cloth is usually protected with a dust-cover.

Altar Cross A crucifix or cross which stands upon the altar or hangs above it.

Altar of Repose See *Place of Reservation*.

Altar Rail The rail or kneelers where the people kneel or stand to receive Communion.

Altar Rail Gates The gates or hinged top of the center of the altar rail. When opened, these allow access to the altar area, and are closed before the administration of Communion.

Ambo See *Lectern* and *Pulpit*.

Amice A large square or rectangular piece of white cloth with strings attached. It is worn under the alb as a hood or over the shoulders. The strings are wound around the neck before being tied around the chest and waist (see *Chapter 4*).

Anthem A text from Scripture or other sources that is sung or said during the liturgy; also called Antiphon.

Anthem at the Fraction The words that are said or sung at the Breaking of the Bread (*BCP, 337 or 364*).

Ascension The Feast commemorating the Ascension of our Lord Jesus Christ to glory. This Feast is forty days after Easter and always occurs on a Thursday.

Ash Wednesday The day of special devotion that marks the beginning of the Lenten observance (see *BCP, 264ff.*; also, *Chapter 18*).

Aspergillum   A branch, brush, or perforated metal globe, with a handle, used for sprinkling holy water.

Assisting Ministers   Persons who assist the celebrant (see *BCP, 322 & 354*).

Aumbry   A receptacle to hold the Reserved Sacrament, that is affixed to a wall, or sits on a shelf apart from an altar (see *Tabernacle*). An aumbry may also be used as a place where chrism and oil are kept; this aumbry is separate from the one used for the Sacrament, and is not identified by the burning of a Sanctuary Lamp.

Baptism   The sacrament of initiation by which a person is born anew by Water and the Holy Spirit and made a member of Christ's Body (see *BCP, 299ff.*; also, *Chapter 16*).

Baptismal Font   The basin or tub for the administration of the Sacrament of Holy Baptism.

Baptismal Water   The water blessed by a bishop or priest for use at Baptism (*BCP, 306*).

Bells   See *Sanctus Bell; Sacristy Bell.*

Benediction   Any blessing by a bishop or priest; or, a service of devotion to Our Lord present in the Blessed Sacrament.

Bier   The stand upon which a casket rests during the Burial of the Dead (see *Chapter 16*).

Bier Lights   Two or more candles that are placed around the coffin or urn at the Burial of the Dead.

Bishop   A successor of the apostles, the chief pastor of a diocese, and (when present) the principal celebrant at sacramental liturgies (see *BCP, 510ff.*).

Bishop's Chair   A chair set apart in cathedrals and some churches, reserved especially for the bishop (sometimes called the Bishop's Throne). Also, a moveable chair or stool (faldstool) used when the bishop is present and sits for various parts of the liturgy (confirmation, ordinations, etc.).

Blessed Sacrament   The consecrated bread and wine of the Eucharist which are the Body and Blood of our Lord Jesus Christ.

Boat   A small container, with a lid and spoon, in which incense is kept before it is placed in the thurible (see *Chapter 13*).

Book of Common Prayer (1979), The   The official liturgy of the Episcopal Church *(BCP)*.

Bread Box   The container in which the bread or hosts for the Eucharist are kept. This is presented to the celebrant at the Offertory by the server or a member of the congregation.

Bucket   A container, equipped with a handle, for Holy Water.

Burse   A pocket or envelope of stiff board covered with material of the same liturgical color as the vestments, in which the corporal is kept when not in use on the altar (see *Chapter 7*).

Candlebearer   See *Torchbearer;* also, *Chapter 11.*

Candle Lighter/Extinguisher   A long pole with a two-pronged end. One side is a tube into which is inserted a taper; a knob is used to raise or lower the taper for lighting of candles. The other side is a bell-shaped snuffer used to extinguish the candles (see *Chapters 5 & 6*).

Candlemas   The Feast of the Presentation of Our Lord in the Temple, February 2nd. The term comes from the tradition of blessing candles on this feast and carrying them in procession as a symbol of the "Light to Lighten the Nations" (see *Nunc Dimittis*).

Canticle   A hymn, usually taken from Scripture, sung or said after the lessons at Morning or Evening Prayer, or as the *Song of Praise* at the Eucharist (see *BCP 144-145* for list).

Cassock   A long garment with sleeves, normally black, worn over street clothes when one serves at the altar. It buttons in the front, and should be long enough to cover the ankles (see *Chapter 4*).

Cassock-Alb   A combination of the amice and alb worn in place of cassock and surplice or amice, alb, and cincture. It is normally white and should be long enough to cover the ankles. A cincture around the waist should be worn with this vestment, although it is not essential. A surplice is not worn over the cassock-alb, but a tunic may be (see *Chapter 4*).

Celebrant   The principal officiant at the Eucharist and other Sacraments. The bishop is the normal celebrant, or, if the bishop is not present, a priest.

Celebrant's Chair   See *Sedilia.*

Censer   See *Thurible.*

Chalice   A metal or ceramic cup into which the wine (and a little water) for the Eucharist is poured.

Chalice Veil   A square piece of material (of the same liturgical color as the vestments) used to cover the chalice and paten when they are not in use. The burse (with the corporal inside) rests on top of the veiled chalice (see *Chapter 7*).

Chancel or **Choir**   The area of the church between the nave and the sanctuary.

Charcoal   Substance upon which incense is burned in the thurible. There are various types of "self-lighting" charcoals (see *Chapter 13*).

Chasuble   A long, wide sleeveless vestment, worn by the celebrant at the Eucharist. It is usually oval when laid out flat, with an opening in the center to accommodate the celebrant's head. It is of the liturgical color of the day or season and usually worn over all other vestments (see *Eucharistic Vestments*).

Choir   A group of singers who assist in the celebration of the liturgy. They may be either in the chancel or in some other part of the church.

Chrism   Oil consecrated by a bishop for use at Baptism *(BCP, 307)*.

Chrismation   The anointing of a person with chrism at Baptism *(BCP, 308)*.

Christmas   The Feast of the Nativity of Our Lord Jesus Christ celebrated on December 25th. The Christmas season extends through January 6, the Feast of the Epiphany.

Church Year   See *BCP, 15ff.;* also *Appendix B.*

Ciborium   A covered metal or ceramic vessel in which the Blessed Sacrament is kept when reserved in a tabernacle or aumbry.

Cincture   A rope, usually white, worn with the alb or cassock-alb, tied with a slip knot at the right side of the waist and allowed to hang down the right side. The ends of the rope may have either knots or tassels. This rope is sometimes called a girdle (see *Chapter 4*).

Coals The burning charcoal in the thurible (see *Chapter 13*).

Collect A prayer that is sung or said on behalf of the people by the celebrant or officiant at liturgical celebrations.

Colors, Liturgical By tradition, various colors are used for the vestments and altar hangings for the different seasons and feasts of the Church Year. In Western use the tradition is:

> *Red*—on Pentecost, Feasts of Martyrs, and during Holy Week.
> *White*—on Feasts of our Lord, Feasts of Saints who were not martyrs, Feasts of the Blessed Virgin Mary, and in some places at the Burial of the Dead.
> *Green*—on the Sundays and Ordinary days of the Year after Epiphany and Pentecost.
> *Blue*—in some places used during Advent.
> *Purple or Violet*—for penitential occasions, during Lent, at Requiems or the Burial of the Dead, and Advent.
> *Black*—in some places for the Burial of the Dead and Requiems.
> *Lenten Array*—in some places used during Lent in place of purple (see *Lenten Array*).

Comfortable Words See *BCP, 332.*

Commendation The rite at the conclusion of the Burial of the Dead *(BCP, 482 or 499).*

Communion Rail See *Altar Rail.*

Communion Rail Gates See *Altar Rail Gates.*

Concelebrant An ordained bishop or priest who celebrates the Eucharist with the principal celebrant.

Confession of Sin A public prayer of penitence at the Eucharist *(BCP, 330, 360, & 393)*, the *Daily Offices* and other times. Also, the Reconciliation of a Penitent (see *BCP, 447ff.*).

Confirmation   A mature public affirmation of the faith and commitment to the responsibilities of one's Baptismal vows, and, the laying on of hands by the bishop (see *BCP, 412ff.*).

Cope   A long cape, worn over the shoulders by the celebrant and others at various liturgies (processions, the Burial of the Dead, etc.), or by a bishop. It is usually of the liturgical color of the day or season, has a clasp at the chest and is worn over alb and stole or over cassock and surplice.

Corporal   A large square white cloth, usually linen, that is placed on the altar at the time of the Offertory and upon which the chalice and paten are placed. The corporal may be kept in the burse when not in use on the altar (see *Chapter 7*).

Credence or **Credence Table**   A shelf or table, usually to the right of the altar, on which the vessels and other items for celebration of the Eucharist are kept (see *Chapter 7*).

Creed   The affirmation of the faith of the Church (see *BCP, 53* for "Apostles' Creed"; *BCP, 326-327* for "Nicene Creed"; and, *BCP, 864* for "Athanasian Creed").

Crossbearer   See *Crucifer.*

Crozier   The bishop's staff representing a shepherd's crook.

Crucifix   A cross upon which a figure of Christ is represented, either crucified or in eucharistic vestments.

Cruets   Glass or metal containers for the wine and water used at the Eucharist. Cruets have handles and tops (either a removable stopper or a lid that can be raised). If the cruets are metal, it is helpful if the wine cruet has a "V" engraved upon it (for "vino"—Latin for wine) and the water cruet an "A" engraved upon it (for "aqua"—Latin for water). This makes for easy identification of the contents. Cruets should be held in the palm of the hand with handles facing out when the celebrant or other person will be pouring (as at the Offertory). When the server is to pour from a cruet (as at the lavabo or ablutions) it should be held by the handle (see *Chapter 9* for illustrations).

Daily Offices   Morning Prayer, Noonday Prayer, Evening Prayer, and Compline (see *Chapter 14* and *BCP, 35ff.*). An Order of Worship for the Evening is also considered an Office (see *Chapter 15* and *BCP, 108ff.*).

Dalmatic   Similar to the tunic and worn by the deacon.

Deacon   An ordained assisting minister whose main functions at the Eucharist are to read the Gospel, (normally lead the Prayers of the People), prepare the gifts at the Offertory, assist with the administration of Communion, help with the ablutions, and dismiss the people. In the absence of a bishop or priest, a deacon may administer Communion from the Reserved Sacrament (*BCP, 408-409*).

Dismissal   The words said or sung by the deacon (or celebrant) at the conclusion of the Eucharist (see *BCP, 339 or 366*). The response to the dismissal is "Thanks be to God" (during the Fifty Days of Easter, "Thanks be to God, alleluia, alleluia.").

Divine Liturgy, The   See *Liturgy;* also, *Eucharist.*

Doxology   Words said or sung in praise of the Holy Trinity (see *Gloria Patri;* also, the conclusion of each Eucharistic Prayer in *BCP*).

Dust-Cover   A cloth placed over the altar cloth at times when the altar is not in use.

Easter   The day celebrating the Lord's Resurrection and the Fifty Days following.

Easter Eve   See *Great Vigil of Easter;* also, *Chapter 18.*

Elements   The bread and wine to be consecrated at the Eucharist.

Elevations   The lifting up of the Consecrated Elements after the Words of Institution, at the conclusion of the Great Thanksgiving, or at the Invitation to Communion.

Epiphany   The Feast of the Manifestation of Our Lord Jesus Christ observed on January 6th. The Epiphany Season continues until the Tuesday before Ash Wednesday.

Epistle   The lesson at the Eucharist preceding the Gospel taken from one of the Letters of the New Testament, the Acts of the Apostles, or the Book of Revelation.

Epistoler   See *Subdeacon.*

Eucharist   The principal act of worship on Sundays and other Feasts (see *Mass, Lord's Supper, Liturgy, The Holy Communion*).

Eucharistic Prayer   That part of the Great Thanksgiving beginning
with the salutation and preface and concluding with the
doxology and Amen. In *The Book of Common Prayer* there
are several Eucharistic Prayers: two for Rite I *(BCP, 333ff. &
340ff.)*; four for Rite II *(BCP, 361ff., 367ff., 369ff., & 372ff.*);
and two forms in An Order for Celebrating the Holy Eucharist
(BCP, 402 & 404).

Eucharistic Vestments   The stole, (maniple), and chasuble worn
by the celebrant at the Eucharist. The stole may either be
worn under the chasuble or, in some places, over it. The
Eucharistic vestments are worn over amice, alb, and cincture,
or over a cassock-alb.

Evensong   Sung Evening Prayer *(BCP, 61ff. or 115ff.)*.

Ewer   See *Flagon*, for water at Baptism or on Maundy Thursday
at the Washing of Feet.

Exsultet   The paean of praise that is sung or said during the first
part of the Great Vigil of Easter by the deacon or other person
appointed *(BCP, 286)*.

Fair Linen   See *Altar Cloth*.

Faldstool   See *Bishop's Chair*.

Fast   A day of special devotion (Ash Wednesday, other weekdays
of Lent and of Holy Week, Good Friday and all other Fridays
of the year, except for Fridays in the Christmas and Easter
seasons, and any Feasts of our Lord which occur on a Friday)
observed by acts of discipline and self-denial.

Feast   A day of celebration associated with the life of Our Lord,
of the Saints, or days of thanksgiving (see *BCP, 15-18*).

Fifty Days of Easter, The   From the Great Vigil of Easter up to
and including the Day of Pentecost.

Flagon   A large metal or ceramic pitcher often used for wine (and
water) to be consecrated at the Eucharist. If more than one
chalice is used during the administration of Communion, the
flagon (or an additional cruet filled with wine and water) is
placed on the altar at the Offertory, and other chalices are
brought to the altar after the Breaking of the Bread. There
should be only one chalice on the altar during the Great

Thanksgiving (see *BCP, 407*).

Font   See *Baptismal Font*; also, a fixed receptacle for holy water at the entrance to the church or in the sacristy.

Frontal   A covering for the altar, usually of the same material as the vestments or of the liturgical color of the season or feast. It may either cover all sides of the altar, or only the front. The altar cloth is spread over the frontal.

Funeral   See *Chapter 16*, The Burial of the Dead.

Genuflection   The bending of the right knee when reverencing the Blessed Sacrament and at other times of solemn reverence (see *Chapter 3*).

Gifts   The offerings of Bread and Wine (and Alms) presented to the celebrant at the Offertory of the Eucharist.

Girdle   See *Cincture*.

Gloria in Excelsis   See *Song of Praise;* also, *BCP, 52, 94, 324, 356.*

Gloria Patri   The Doxology which concludes the recitation of a psalm at the beginning of the Eucharist; at the end of the psalms in the Daily Offices; and at other times as listed in the Prayer Book (see *BCP, 63*).

Good Friday   The Friday before Easter Day on which the Passion and Death of our Lord Jesus Christ is celebrated (see *BCP, 276ff.*; also, *Chapter 18*).

Gospel   The final lesson in The Word of God taken from one of the four Gospels in the New Testament. It is normally read by a deacon or priest, and as a sign of reverence, the people and assisting ministers stand when the Gospel is proclaimed (see *BCP, 326 or 357*).

Gospel Book   The book (usually with an ornamented cover) which contains the Gospel lessons appointed for use at the Eucharist. It is carried in procession (at the entrance) and at the proclamation of the Gospel by the deacon or other reader. "It is desirable that the lessons and Gospel be read from a book or books of appropriate size and dignity" *(BCP, 406)*.

Gospeller   See *Deacon.*

Gospel Procession   The movement of the deacon (or celebrant) with torches (incense and processional cross) to the place of the proclamation of the Gospel (the nave, the lectern, or the pulpit).

Gradual Psalm   The psalm appointed to be read or sung after the lesson at the celebration of the Eucharist (see *BCP, 326, 357, & 889-931*).

Great Thanksgiving, The   The major prayer of the Eucharist beginning with the salutation and preface and concluding with the Lord's Prayer (see *BCP, 333ff., 361ff.*).

Holy Communion, The   The second part of the Holy Eucharist, following the Word of God and beginning with the Offertory (see *BCP, 333ff., 361ff.*). This term may also refer to the whole service in the same way as Mass, Lord's Supper, Holy Eucharist, or Divine Liturgy.

Holy Saturday   See *Chapter 18* and *BCP, 283;* also, see *Great Vigil of Easter.*

Holy Water   Water blessed by a bishop or priest for use in blessing the people, in the setting apart of objects for use in the church, or for other liturgical purposes. Holy Water is often used at the Burial of the Dead (see *Chapter 16*), at Weddings (see *Chapter 16*), and at other times at the discretion of the priest.

Holy Week   The week that commemorates our Lord's Passion and Death: The Sunday of the Passion: Palm Sunday; Monday, Tuesday, and Wednesday of Holy Week; Maundy Thursday; Good Friday; and, Holy Saturday (see *BCP, 270-283;* also, *Chapter 18*). The Great Vigil of Easter is the climax of Holy Week and the beginning of the Fifty Days of Easter celebrating the Resurrection of our Lord.

Hymn   Sacred poetry set to music and sung during the liturgy.

Incense   A mixture of perfumed spices, burned on the coals in the thurible, and used as a sign of prayer, honor, and solemnity at liturgical functions (see *Chapter 13*).

Introit   The hymn, psalm, or anthem sung (or said) at the entrance of the ministers at the Eucharist *(BCP, 323 or 355)*.

Invitatory   At Morning Prayer: the Venite, Psalm 95, Jubilate, or Christ our Passover; at Evening Prayer: O Gracious Light

(Phos Hilaron) or other suitable hymn or psalm. The invitatory is used at the beginning of an Office after the opening versicle and response and before the appointed psalms.

Kneeling   A posture signifying reverence or penitence (see *Chapter 3*).

Kyrie Eleison   See *Song of Praise*; also, *BCP, 324, 356 or 389ff.*

Lavabo   The washing of the celebrant's fingers after the Offertory at the Eucharist or at other times such as when oil or chrism is used or after the imposition of ashes on Ash Wednesday (see *Chapter 9*).

Lavabo Bowl   The metal or ceramic dish into which the water is poured by the server at the lavabo.

Lavabo Towel   A piece of cloth, usually linen, presented to the celebrant by the server at the lavabo to dry the fingers. It is presented hung over the server's left arm.

Lay Reader   A person licensed by the Bishop to read the lessons at the Eucharist or at the Daily Offices and who may assist the celebrant or officiant in other ways; if specifically licensed by the Bishop, may administer the chalice at Communion.

Lectern   The book-stand or podium from which the lessons and sometimes the Gospel are read at the Eucharist and other Offices. Also called an Ambo.

Lectionary   The appointed lessons and psalms for use at the Eucharist and Daily Offices (see *BCP, 888ff.*).

Lector   A person who reads a lesson at the liturgy.

Lent   The season of penitence and preparation for Holy Week and Easter which begins on Ash Wednesday (see *BCP, 264-65*).

Lenten Array   In some places, the use of sack-cloth or similar fabric in place of purple for vestments, coverings, and hangings during Lent and Holy Week.

Lenten Cross   In some places, a plain wooden processional cross (painted red with black edges) used during Lent and Holy Week.

Lesser Feasts and Fasts   A book containing the collects, lessons, psalms, and short biographical material for the minor saints' days and observances found in the calendar of *The Book of Common Prayer.*

Lesson   The first reading from scripture at the Eucharist; also, the scripture readings at the Daily Offices or at other liturgies.

Litany   Any form of prayer with petitions and responses; the Great Litany (see *BCP, 148ff.*; also, *Chapter 17*).

Liturgical Colors   See *Colors, Liturgical.*

Liturgy   The "work of the people." In Western usage this term may apply to any public celebration of the Church. In the Churches of the East, The Divine Liturgy refers specifically to the celebration of the Holy Eucharist.

Lord's Supper, The   The celebration of the Holy Eucharist.

Lord's Table, The   See *Altar.*

Magnificat   The song of Mary (Luke 1:46-55) normally used as one of the canticles at Evening Prayer; also, may be used as a Song of Praise on Feasts of St. Mary or at other times (see *BCP, 65 or 119*).

Maniple   A band of cloth worn, in some places, over the left arm by the celebrant at the Eucharist. It is of the same liturgical color as the stole and chasuble (see *Eucharistic Vestments*).

Mass   The celebration of the Holy Eucharist.

Master of Ceremonies   A person designated to direct the ceremonial at the liturgy.

Matins   Morning Prayer.

Maundy   See *Washing of Feet;* also, *BCP, 274* and *Chapter 18.*

Maundy Thursday   Thursday in Holy Week (see *BCP, 274;* also, *Chapter 18*).

Ministers   The celebrant, officiant and any others (lay persons or ordained) who assist in the celebration of the liturgy.

Missal   See *Altar Book.*

Missal Stand   The stand (or, in some places, a pillow) upon which the Altar Book rests when in use at the altar.

Mitre   The triangular-shaped head covering worn by a bishop.

Monstrance   A receptacle for the Blessed Sacrament used at Benediction.

Nave   The area of the church where the people gather for the liturgy.

Nunc Dimittis   The Song of Simeon (Luke 2:29-32) normally used as one of the canticles at Evening Prayer and Compline (see *BCP, 66, 120, & 135*). This canticle is also used at Candlemas.

Occasional Services, Book of   A book containing optional services and prayers authorized for use by the Episcopal Church.

Offertory   The presentation, reception, preparation, and offering of the gifts at the beginning of The Holy Communion, the second part of the Eucharist.

Offertory Sentence   A passage of scripture that may be said or sung at the beginning or during the Offertory (see *BCP, 333 or 361*).

Offertory Procession   At the Eucharist, the presentation of the bread, wine, and other gifts by members of the congregation.

Office   See *Daily Offices.*

Officiant   A person who officiates at the Daily Offices and other rites.

Oil   A liquid substance blessed by a bishop or priest for use in the Ministration to the Sick (*BCP, 455*). See also *Chrism.*

Pall   A stiffened square of linen (or other) white cloth that is placed over the chalice to keep objects from falling into the wine. The term may refer also to the cloth covering the casket or urn during the Burial of the Dead.

Palm Sunday   The Sunday of the Passion (see *BCP, 270-73;* also, *Chapter 18*).

Palms   Branches blessed at the Palm Sunday Liturgy and carried by the people in procession (see *Chapter 17*).

Paschal Candle   A large white candle, which may be decorated with a cross, the year of blessing, A (alpha) and Ω (omega), grains of incense, and other symbols of the resurrection. It is lighted at the beginning of the Great Vigil of Easter and burns for all services during the Fifty Days of Easter. At other times, it may be kept near the Baptismal Font and lighted for Baptisms. It may also be carried in procession at the Burial of the Dead, and placed in its holder near the casket or urn.

Paschal Candlestand   A large wooden or metal stand in which the Paschal candle is placed. The stand rests on the floor, and is of such height that the candle is prominent.

Passion Week   See *Holy Week.*

Paten   A metal or ceramic plate on which the bread for the Eucharist is placed after it is presented by the server or a member of the congregation.

Penance   See *Confession of Sin*; also *BCP, 446-52.*

Pentecost, Day of   The conclusion of the Fifty Days of Easter and the commemoration of the descent of the Holy Spirit upon the disciples.

Pentecost, Season of   The Sundays and Weekdays following the Day of Pentecost and ending on the Saturday before the First Sunday of Advent.

Phos Hilaron   See *Invitatory;* also *BCP, 64, 112, & 118.*

Piscina   A sink for washing the vessels used at the Eucharist and for reverently disposing of Wine that has been consecrated. The piscina does not drain into a sewer or disposal system, but directly into the ground.

Place of Reservation   The altar or other place apart from the main altar of the church where the Blessed Sacrament is reserved on Maundy Thursday for use at the Good Friday Liturgy. Also called Altar of Repose (see *Chapter 18*; also, *Aumbry, Tabernacle*).

Post Communion   The Prayer of Thanksgiving after Holy Communion (see *BCP, 339, 365-66*). There are also proper Post Communion prayers appointed for various occasions.

Prayers of the People   See *BCP, 328, 359, and 383ff.*

Preface   The first part of The Great Thanksgiving up to the Sanctus. Proper Prefaces are appointed for certain occasions (see *BCP, 344-49 or 377-82*).

President's Chair   See *Sedilia.*

Procession   See *Chapter 17.*

Processional Cross   A metal or wooden cross or crucifix affixed to a pole and carried in processions. See also *Lenten Cross.*

Psalm   A portion from the ancient Jewish hymn book found in Scripture (The Book of Psalms) and in *The Book of Common Prayer* (see *BCP, 585-808*).

Pulpit   The place from which the sermon is preached and from which the Gospel may be read. Also called an Ambo.

Purificator   A linen (or other) white cloth used for cleansing the chalice during the ablutions, or for wiping the chalice during the administration of Communion (see *Chapters 3 and 9*).

Pyx   A receptacle for reserving the Blessed Sacrament for use in Communion of the Sick.

Requiem   A celebration of the Eucharist for the commemoration of the dead.

Reserved Sacrament   The consecrated Bread and Wine reserved for administration to the sick or others who could not attend the celebration of the Eucharist.

Reverence (of the Altar or the Blessed Sacrament)   A genuflection or solemn bow.

Rite I   The liturgies in *The Book of Common Prayer* that are in traditional language.

Rite II   The liturgies in *The Book of Common Prayer* that are in modern language.

Rubric   The ceremonial and other directions found printed in italics in *The Book of Common Prayer.* The word comes from the Latin for "red" since the directions were traditionally printed in that color.

Sacrament Lamp   A clear or white container with oil or a candle that burns in front of or near the place where the Blessed Sacrament is reserved. This candle is never extinguished when the Sacrament is present. The Sacrament Lamp may also be known as the Sanctuary Lamp or Light.

Sacristy   A room or rooms where the vessels, vestments, and other liturgical objects are kept, and where the celebrant, officiants, and assistants vest before the liturgy.

Sacristy Bell   A bell in the sacristy rung at the entrance of the ministers.

Sanctuary   The area of the church surrounding the altar.

Sanctuary Lamp or Light   See *Sacrament Lamp.*

Sanctus   The acclamation "Holy, holy, holy . . ." sung or said at the conclusion of the Preface of the Great Thanksgiving *(BCP, 334, 341, 362ff.)*.

Sanctus Bell   A bell or set of bells in the sanctuary (or in a tower) that is rung or struck during the sanctus, elevations, and at other times.

Sedilia   The chair from which the celebrant presides at the Word of God. In some places, this may be called the President's Chair. It is usually flanked by chairs for the assisting ministers and others.

Sequence Hymn   A hymn sung between the Epistle and Gospel (after the Alleluia Verse or Tract) which normally relates to the lessons appointed for the day.

Server   One who assists at the altar.

Shell, Baptismal   The metal or ceramic cup or dish used to pour water during the administration of Holy Baptism.

Sign of the Cross   The tracing on one's forehead, chest and shoulders of the outline of the Cross (see *Chapter 3*).

Simple Bow   The inclination of one's head and shoulders as a sign of respect (see *Chapter 3*).

Solemn Bow   An inclination from the waist as a sign of reverence (see *Chapter 3*).

Solemn Procession   See *Chapter 17.*

Song of Praise   The hymn or canticle at the beginning of the Eucharist following the Acclamation (see *BCP, 324 or 356*).

Spoon   A utensil used with the boat to place incense on the hot coals in the thurible (see *Chapter 13*).

Staff, Pastoral   See *Crozier.*

Stand   See *Missal Stand.*

Station   In a solemn procession, a place where a pause is made for a versicle, response, and collect, such as at the creche at Christmas, at the entrance to the church on Palm Sunday (*BCP 271-72),* or at the Baptismal Font on the Day of Pentecost (see *Chapter 17).*

Stations of the Cross   See *Way of the Cross.*

Steps, Altar   The one or more steps leading up to the altar.

Stole   A long strip of material worn by bishops, priests, and deacons when officiating at the Eucharist or other sacramental functions. The priest wears the stole around the neck and hanging down in front (either crossed or straight) over an alb or surplice. The deacon wears the stole over the left shoulder and crossed under the right arm, again either over an alb or surplice. The stole is of the liturgical color of the day and matches the material of the other vestments (see *Eucharistic Vestments).*

Stripping of the Altars   On Maundy Thursday; see *Chapter 18.*

Subdeacon   A lay person who assists the deacon and celebrant, and normally reads the epistle at the Eucharist.

Sunday of the Passion, The   Palm Sunday (see *Chapter 18).*

Surplice   An ample white vestment worn over a cassock. It has full sleeves, a round or square yoke (neck), and is at least mid-calf in length (see *Chapter 4).*

Tabernacle   A box or receptacle for the Reserved Sacrament located on an altar (see also *Aumbry).*

Taper   A long narrow wax-covered wick that is put into the candle lighter; or, a small candle for use by members of the congregation at vigils and other services; also, any candle (see *Chapters 5 & 6* concerning candles).

Te Deum   A canticle used at Morning Prayer, as a Song of Praise at the Eucharist, or added to a service on days of special Thanksgiving (see *BCP, 52 or 95).*

Throne   A term sometimes used for the Bishop's Chair.

Thurible   The container in which incense is burned (see *Chapter 13).*

Thurifer   The server whose duty it is to handle the thurible and boat (see *Chapter 13*).

Tongs   A two-pronged hand-held device for holding charcoal when lighting (see *Chapter 13*).

Torch   A candle on a pole or stand that is carried by an acolyte (see *Chapter 11*).

Torchbearers   Acolytes who carry torches or processional candles (see *Chapter 11*).

Towel   A cloth used to wipe the celebrant's hands, also called the lavabo towel.

Tract   A sentence of scripture sung or said in place of the alleluia verse during Lent.

Tunic or Tunicle   A vestment with ample sleeves worn over an alb or cassock alb of the same liturgical color as the vestments of the celebrant or some other festive color. This vestment is usually worn by the subdeacon, and may be worn by the crucifer on festive occasions (see *Chapter 4*).

Urn   A receptacle containing the remains of a body that has been cremated.

Veil   A covering (see *Chalice Veil*).

Venite   See *Invitatory;* also, *BCP, 44, 82 or 146.*

Veneration of the Cross   On Good Friday, after the cross has been brought into the church, it may either be venerated while all kneel in place or each person may come forward individually to venerate the cross (see *BCP, 281ff.*; also *Chapter 18*). In some places, the veneration is an act of kissing the foot of the cross.

Versicle   A short sentence, often taken from the Psalms, sung or said at the liturgy and followed by a response from the people.

Vessels, Sacred   See *Chalice; Paten; Ciborium; Flagon.*

Vesting   See *Chapter 4.*

Vestment   Any article of clothing worn over street clothes by those officiating or assisting at liturgical celebrations.

Vigils   A period or service of preparation before major festivals or celebrations (see Great Vigil of Easter, *BCP, 284ff.*; Vigil of Pentecost, *BCP, 227*; also *Chapter 18*).

Washing of Altars   In some places, this act is performed by ministers and servers after the stripping of the altars on Maundy Thursday.

Washing of Feet   The rite performed on Maundy Thursday commemorating Our Lord's washing of the feet of the apostles at the Last Supper (see *BCP, 274;* also *Chapter 17*).

Watch (before the Blessed Sacrament)   The vigil kept at the Place of Reservation after the Maundy Thursday liturgy.

Way of the Cross   A Procession with stations commemorating the Passion and Death of Our Lord Jesus Christ.

Wedding   The Celebration and Blessing of a Marriage (see *BCP, 423ff.;* also, *Chapter 16*).

Word of God, The   The first part of the Holy Eucharist ending with the Peace. The focus of this part of the Eucharist is on the reading of Scripture and prayers of praise and petition.

Words of Institution   That part of the Eucharistic Prayer recalling the words and actions of Our Lord at the Last Supper.

Year, Church   See *Appendix B.*

NOTES